POOR RICHARD'S
QUOTATIONS

POOR RICHARD'S
QUOTATIONS

Being a

Collection of Quotations

from

POOR RICHARD ALMANACKS

Published by Benjamin Franklin

in the

Years of our LORD

1733 through 1758

Blue Mountain Arts inc.

The *linecuts* used throughout this book are
based on the original *linecuts* used by Benjamin
Franklin in the POOR RICHARD ALMANACKS.

Selected and Designed by Dr. Stephen Schutz

Library of Congress Catalog Card Number: 75-18836
ISBN Number: 0-88396-013-3

Manufactured in the United States of America

First Printing, July, 1975.
Second Printing, October, 1975.
Third Printing, March, 1976.

Blue Mountain Arts inc.
P.O. Box 4549   Boulder, Colorado 80302

INTRODUCTION

Besides the usual Things expected in an Almanack, I hope the profess'd Teachers of Mankind will excuse my scattering here and there some instructive Hints in Matters of Morality and Religion. And be not thou disturbed, O grave and sober Reader, if among the more serious Sentences in my Book, thou findest me trifling now and then, and talking idly. In all the Dishes I have hitherto cook'd for thee, there is solid Meat enough for thy Money. There are Scraps from the Table of Wisdom, that will if well digested, yield strong Nourishment to thy Mind. But squeamish Stomachs cannot eat without Pickles; which, 'tis true are good for nothing else, but they provoke an Appetite. The Vain Youth that reads my Almanack for the sake of an idle Joke, will perhaps meet with a serious Reflection, that he may ever after be the better for.

Benjamin Franklin

From the introduction to
Poor Richard's Almanack, 1739

Early to bed and early to rise,
makes a man healthy, wealthy and wise.

An ill Wound,
but not an ill Name,
may be healed.

There is much difference between
imitating a good man, and counterfeiting him.

God helps them that help themselves.

What signifies knowing the Names,
if you know not the Natures of things.

One Today is worth two Tomorrows.

He that's content hath enough;
He that complains, has too much.

If you would be loved, love and be loveable.

Silence is not always a Sign of Wisdom,
but Babbling is ever a Mark of Folly.

Being ignorant is not so much a Shame,
as being unwilling to learn.

Fools need Advice most, but wise Men only are
the better for it.

'Tis easy to frame a good, bold resolution;
But hard is the Task that concerns execution.

Time was my spouse and I could not agree,
Striving about superiority:
The text which saith that man and wife are one,
Was the chief argument we stood upon:
She held, they both one woman should become;
I held they should be man, and both but one.
Thus we contended daily, but the strife
Could not be ended, till both were one Wife.

Now I've a sheep and a cow,
everybody bids me good morrow.

He that can have Patience, can have what he will.

A Flatterer never seems absurd:
The Flattered always take his Word.

Ever you remark another's Sin,
Bid your own Conscience look within.

Quarrels never could last long,
If on one side only lay the wrong.

He that hath a Trade, hath an Estate.

Beware of meat twice boil'd,
and an old Foe reconcil'd.

He's the best physician that knows
the worthlessness of the most medicines.

He is ill cloth'd, who is bare of Virtue.

What Death is, dost thou ask of me;
    Till dead I do not know;
Come to me when thou hear'st I'm dead;
    Then what 'tis I shall show.
To die's to cease to be, it seems,
    So Learned Seneca did think;
But we've Philosophers of modern Date,
    Who say 'tis Death to cease to Drink.

Plough deep; while Sluggards sleep;
And you shall have Corn, to sell and to keep.

Distrust and caution are the parents of security.

'Tis easy to see, hard to foresee.

Whimsical Will once fancied he was ill,
The Doctor's call'd, who thus examin'd Will;
How is your Appetite? O, as to that
I eat right heartily, you see I'm fat.
How is your Sleep anights? 'Tis sound and good;
I eat, drink, sleep as well as e'er I cou'd.
Well, says the Doctor, clapping on his Hat;
I'll give you something shall remove all that.

None preaches better than the ant,
and she says nothing.

There's more old Drunkards than old Doctors.

The absent are never without fault,
nor the present without excuse.

God heals, and the Doctor takes the Fees.

If you desire many things,
many things will seem but a few.

He that scatters thorns, let him not go barefoot.

Do good to thy Friend to keep him,
to thy enemy to gain him.

The greatest monarch on the proudest throne,
is oblig'd to sit upon his own arse.

The worst wheel of the cart
makes the most noise.

No better relation than a prudent and faithful Friend.

He that can compose himself,
is wiser than he that composes books.

Hunger never saw bad bread.

Three may keep a Secret,
if two of them are dead.

In Christendom we all are Christians now,
And thus I answer, if you ask me how;
Where with Christ's Rule our Lives will not comply,
We bend it like a Rule of Lead, say I;
Making it thus comply with what we be,
And only thus our Lives with th' Rule agree.

If thou hast wit and learning,
add to it Wisdom and Modesty.

Drive thy business;
let not it drive thee.

Sell not virtue to purchase wealth,
nor Liberty to purchase power.

A false Friend and a Shadow,
attend only while the Sun shines.

Haste makes Waste.

He that falls in love with himself,
will have no Rivals.

A lawyer being sick and extreamly ill
Was moved by his Friends to make his Will;
Which soon he did, gave all the Wealth he had
To frantic Persons, lunatick and mad;
And to his Friends this Reason did reveal
(That they might see with Equity he'd deal).
From Madmen's Hands I did my Wealth receive,
Therefore that Wealth to Madmen's Hands I leave.

Knowledge like a rich Soil,
feeds if not a world of Corn,
a world of Weeds.

A wise Man will desire no more,
than what he may get justly,
use soberly, distribute chearfully,
and leave contently.

Avoid dishonest Gain; No price
Can recompense the Pangs of Vice.

Fear to do ill,
and you need fear nought else.

Idleness is the Dead Sea, that swallows all Virtues:
Be active in Business, that Temptation may miss her Aim:
The Bird that sits, is easily shot.

He that spills the Rum,
loses that only; He that drinks it,
often loses both that and himself.

A man is never so ridiculous by those qualities that
are his own as by those that he affects to have.

The Things which hurt, instruct.

Fear not Death; for the sooner we die,
the longer shall we be immortal.

Well done is better than well said.

Tomorrow, every Fault is to be amended;
but that Tomorrow never comes.

Simplicity, Innocence, Industry, Temperance, are Arts
that lead to Tranquility, as much as Learning,
Knowledge, Wisdom and Contemplation. A noble
Simplicity in Discourse is a Talent rare, and above the
Reach of ordinary Men. Genius, Fancy, Learning,
Memory, etc. are so far from helping, that they often
hinder the Attaining of it ... By the Word Simplicity, is
not always meant Folly or Ignorance; but often, pure and
upright Nature, free from Artifice, Craft or deceitful
Ornament.

The Benefit of going to LAW

Two Beggars travelling along,
    One blind, the other lame,
Pick'd up an Oyster on the Way
    To which they both laid claim:
The Matter rose so high, that they
    Resolv'd to go to Law,
As often richer Fools have done,
    Who quarrel for a Straw.
A Lawyer took it straight in hand,
    Who knew his Business was,
To mind nor one nor the others side,
    But make the best of the Cause;
As always in the Law's the Case:
    So he his Judgment gave,
And Lawyer-like he thus resolv'd
    What each of them should have;
        Blind Plaintif, lame Defendant, share
        The Friendly Laws impartial Case,
        A Shell for him, a Shell for thee,
        The Middle is the Lawyer's Fee.

Men take more pains to mask than mend.

He that lies down with Dogs,
shall rise up with fleas.

Diligence is the Mother of Good-Luck.

Let no Pleasure tempt thee, no Profit allure
thee, no Ambition corrupt thee, no Example
sway thee, no Persuasion move thee, to do
anything which thou knowest to be Evil; So
shalt thou always live jollily: for a good
Conscience is a continual Christmas. Adieu.

Laws too gentle are seldom obeyed;
too severe, seldom executed.

Whate'er's desired, Knowledge, Fame, or Pelf,
Not one will change his Neighbour with himself.
The learn'd are happy Nature to explore,
The Fool is happy that he knows no more.
The Rich are happy in the Plenty given;
The Poor contents him with the Care of Heav'n.
Thus does some Comfort ev'ry State attend.
And Pride's bestow'd on all, a common Friend.

He doest not possess Wealth,
it possesses him.

Altho' thy Teacher act not as he preaches,
Yet nevertheless, if good, do what he teaches;
Good Counsel, failing Men may give; for why,
He that's aground knows where the Shoal doth lie.
My old Friend Berryman, oft, when alive,
Taught others Thrift; himself could never thrive:
Thus like the Whetstone, many Men are wont
To sharpen others while themselves are blunt.

There's many witty men whose
brains can't fill their bellies.

A learned blockhead is a greater blockhead
than an ignorant one.

'Tis against some Men's Principle to pay Interest,
and seems against other's Interest to pay the Principal.

A Lie stands on one leg,
Truth on two.

He that is of Opinion Money will do every Thing,
may well be suspected of doing every Thing for Money.

Mankind are very odd Creatures:
One half censure what they practice,
the other half practice what they censure;
the rest always say and do as they ought.

Who is wise?
He that learns from every One.
Who is powerful?
He that governs his Passions.
Who is rich?
He that is content.
Who is that?
Nobody.

Nothing humbler than Ambition,
when it is about to climb.

The Doors of Wisdom are never shut.

If Man could have Half his Wishes,
he would double his Troubles.

Be slow in choosing a Friend,
slower in changing.

He is Governor that governs his Passions,
and he a Servant that serves them.

These reproductions of actual pages from POOR RICHARD'S ALMANACK show how Franklin used every possible space to fit in his sayings.

NOVEMBER. *IX Month.*

She longs to wake, and wiſhes to get free,
To launch from Earth into ETERNITY.
For while the boundleſs Theme extends our Thought,
Ten thouſand thouſand rolling Years are nought.
O endleſs Thought! divine *Eternity!*
Th'immortal Soul ſhares but a Part of thee;
For thou wert preſent when our Life began,
When the warm Duſt ſhot up in breathing Man. Ere

		Remark. days, &c.	☉ riſ	☉ ſet	☽ pl.	Aſpects, &c.
1	6	All Saints.	7 3	4 57	♍ 21	*Not to overſee*
2	7	All Souls.	7 4	4 56	♎ 4	*Workmen, is to*
3	F	22 paſt Trin.	7 5	4 55	16	△ ☉ ♂ *leave*
4	2	*pleaſant,*	7 6	4 54	28	☽ with ♀ *them*
5	3	Powder Plot.	7 7	4 53	♏ 10	☽ with ☿ *your*
6	4	*wind and*	7 8	4 52	22	♂ ſou. 8 5
7	5	Day 9 42	7 9	4 51	♐ 4	♃ riſes 5 35
8	6	Days dec. 5 10	7 10	4 50	15	☽ with ♄ *Purſe*
9	7	*rain, with*	7 11	4 49	27	Sirius riſes 9 47
10	F	23 paſt Trin.	7 12	4 48	♑ 9	*open.*
11	2	*moderace*	7 12	4 48	21	☉ in ♐
12	3	*weather ;*	7 13	4 47	♒ 3	♀ riſes 4 42
13	4	*then*	7 14	4 46	15	△ ♂ ☿
14	5	Day 9 30 long.	7 15	4 45	28	*The Wiſe and*
15	6	*clouds,*	7 16	4 44	♓ 11	*Brave dares*
16	7	*wind*	7 16	4 44	24	☽ with ♂ *own*
17	F.	24 paſt Trin.	7 17	4 43	♈ 8	☍ ☉ ♃ *that he*
18	2	*and rain,*	7 18	4 42	22	Sirius riſe 9 8
19	3	Days 9 24 long.	7 18	4 42	♉ 7	☍ ♃ ☿ *was*
20	4	*if not*	7 19	4 41	22	7 *s ſou. 11 0
21	5	*ſnow ;*	7 19	4 41	♊ 7	☽ w. ♃ *wrong.*
22	6	Days dec. 5 30	7 20	4 40	22	☌ ☉ ☿ *Cunning*
23	7	*cold and*	7 20	4 40	♋ 7	♃ ſou. 11 35
24	F	25 paſt Trin.	7 21	4 39	22	*proceeds from*
25	2	*clear,*	7 22	4 38	♌ 7	♀ riſes 4 1
26	3	Days 9 16 long.	7 22	4 38	21	♂ ſou. 7 12
27	4	*follow'd by*	7 23	4 37	♍ 4	☌ ☉ ♄ *Want*
28	5	Days dec. 5 36	7 23	4 37	17	Sirius riſe 8 25
29	6	*clouds and ſnow*	7 24	4 36	♎ 0	*of Capacity.*
30	7	St. ANDREW.	7 24	4 36	13	7*s ſou. 10 16
		or rain.				

POOR RICHARD'S ALMANACK 1751

1751. NOVEMBER hath xxx Days

	D.	H.
New ☽	6	7 aft.
First Q.	14	10 aft
Full ●	21	5 aft
Last Q.	28	at noon.

☊			
1	♐	3	Deg
11		3	
21		3	

Planets Places.

D.	☉	♄	♃	♂	♀	☿	☽L
	♏	♐	♊	♓	♏	♏	
1	20	13	8	22	2	7	S. 5
6	25	14	8	23	1	15	1
11	♐ 0	14	7	25	1	23	N 4
16	5	15	6	27	2	♐ 1	5
21	10	16	6	29	3	9	S. 0
26	15	16	5	♈ 2	5	17	5

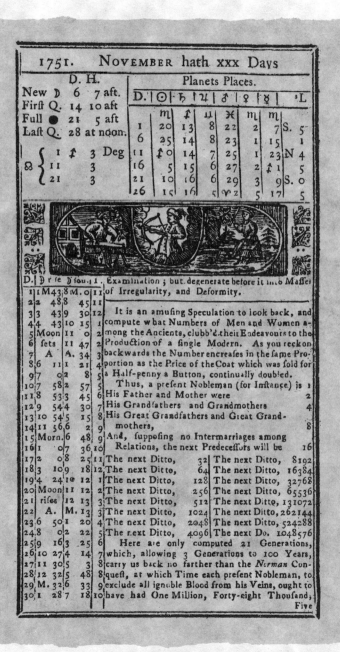

D.	☽ rise	☽ sou.	I.
1	1 M 43	8 M. 0	11
2	2 48	8 45	11
3	3 43	9 30	12
4	4 43	10 15	1
5	Moon	11 0	2
6	sets	11 47	2
7	A	A. 34	3
8	6 11	1 21	4
9	7 0	2 8	5
10	7 58	2 57	5
11	8 53	3 45	6
12	9 54	4 30	7
13	10 54	5 15	8
14	11 56	6 2	9
15	Morn.	6 48	9
16	1 0	7 36	10
17	2 0	8 25	11
18	3 10	9 18	12
19	4 24	10 12	1
20	Moon	11 12	2
21	rises	12 13	3
22	A.	M. 13	3
23	6 50	1 20	4
24	8 0	2 22	5
25	9 16	3 25	6
26	10 27	4 14	7
27	11 30	5 3	8
28	12 32	5 48	8
29	M. 32	6 33	9
30	1 28	7 18	10

Examination; but degenerate before it into Masses of Irregularity, and Deformity.

It is an amusing Speculation to look back, and compute what Numbers of Men and Women among the Ancients, clubb'd their Endeavours to the Production of a single Modern. As you reckon backwards the Number encreases in the same Proportion as the Price of the Coat which was sold for a Half-penny a Button, continually doubled.

Thus, a present Nobleman (for Instance) is	1
His Father and Mother were	2
His Grandfathers and Grandmothers	4
His Great Grandfathers and Great Grandmothers,	8
And, supposing no Intermarriages among Relations, the next Predecessors will be	16

The next Ditto,	32	The next Ditto,	8192
The next Ditto,	64	The next Ditto,	16384
The next Ditto,	128	The next Ditto,	32768
The next Ditto,	256	The next Ditto,	65536
The next Ditto,	512	The next Ditto,	131072
The next Ditto,	1024	The next Ditto,	262144
The next Ditto,	2048	The next Ditto,	524288
The next Ditto,	4096	The next Do.	1048576

Here are only computed 21 Generations, which, allowing 3 Generations to 100 Years, carry us back no farther than the *Norman* Conquest, at which Time each present Nobleman, to exclude all ignoble Blood from his Veins, ought to have had One Million, Forty-eight Thousand, Five

POOR RICHARD'S ALMANACK 1751

DECEMBER. *X Month.*

Ere the Foundations of the World were laid,
Ere kindling Light th'Almighty Word obey'd,
Thou wert; and when the ſubterraneous Flame,
Shall burſt its Priſon, and devour this Frame,
From angry Heav'n when the keen Lightning flies,
When fervent Heat diſſolves the melting Skies,
Thou ſtill ſhalt be; ſtill as thou wert before,
And know no Change when *Time* ſhall be no more.

		Remark. days, &c.	☉ riſ	☉ ſet	☽ pl.	Aſpects, &c.
1	F	Advent Sunday.	7 24	4 36	♎ 25	✱ ♃ ♂ *The*
2	2	*pleaſant for*	7 24	4 36	♏ 7	☽ with ♀ *Proud*
3	3	*the ſeaſon,*	7 25	4 35	19	Sirius riſe 8 3
4	4	Day 9 10 long.	7 25	4 35	♐ 1	7 *s ſou 10 0
5	5	Days dec. 5 40.	7 25	4 35	13	☽ with ♄ *hate*
6	6	*then clouds*	7 25	4 35	24	♂ ſou 6 48
7	7	*with rain,*	7 25	4 35	♑ 6	☽ with ☿ *Pride*
8	F	Concep. V. M.	7 25	4 35	18	♃ ſou 10 22
9	2	*or ſnow,*	7 25	4 35	♒ 0	—*in others.*
10	3	Shorteſt day 9 9	7 25	4 35	12	☉ in ♑
11	4	*mode-*	7 25	4 35	25	□ ♂ ☿ *Who*
12	5	*rate wea-*	7 25	4 35	♓ 8	Sirius riſe 7 23
13	6	St. Lucy.	7 25	4 35	21	♀ riſe 3 37
14	7	*ther; then*	7 25	4 35	♈ 4	*judges beſt of a*
15	F	3 in Advent.	7 25	4 35	17	☽ with ♂ *Man,*
16	2	*cold, with*	7 25	4 35	♉ 1	7*s ſou. 9 4
17	3	*clouds.*	7 25	4 35	16	✱ ♀ ☿ *his*
18	4	Fmber Week.	7 25	4 35	♊ 1	☽ with ♃ *Ene-*
19	5	Day inc. 2 m.	7 24	4 36	16	*mies or himſelf?*
20	6	*and falling*	7 24	4 36	♋ 1	*Drunkenneſs,*
21	7	St. THOMAS.	7 24	4 36	16	*that worſt of E-*
22	F	4 in Advent.	7 24	4 36	♌ 1	Sirius riſes 6 40
23	2	*weather,*	7 23	4 37	15	*vils, makes ſome*
24	3	*wind and*	7 23	4 37	29	*Men Fools, ſome*
25	4	CHRIST born	7 23	4 37	♍ 13	*Beaſts, ſome De-*
26	5	St. STEPHEN.	7 22	4 38	27	♂ ſo. 5 57 *vils.*
27	6	St. JOHN. *ſnow*	7 22	4 38	♎ 9	♀ r. 2 55 *'Tis not*
28	7	Innocents. *or*	7 21	4 39	21	□ ☉ ♂ *a Holi-*
29	F	*cold rain.*	7 21	4 39	♏ 3	7 *s ſo. 8 6 *day*
30	2	Day inc. 10 m.	7 20	4 40	15	*that's not kept*
31	3	Silveſter.	7 19	4 41	27	♃ ſo. 8 25 *holy.*

POOR RICHARD'S ALMANACK 1751

1751. DECEMBER hath XXXI Days.

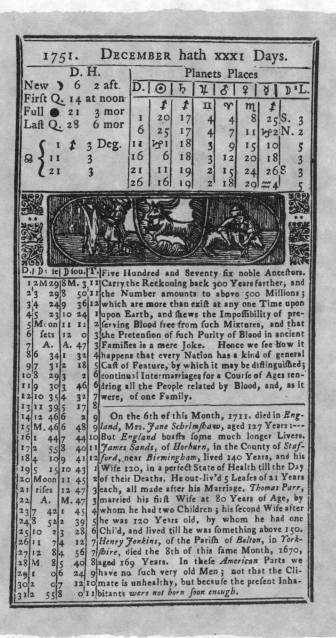

	D.	H.
New ☽	6	2 aft.
First Q.	14	at noon
Full ●	21	3 mor
Last Q.	28	6 mor

☊ { 1 ♐ 3 Deg.
11 3
21 3 }

Planets Places

D.	☉	♄	♃	♂	♀	☿	☽'s L.
	♐	♐	♊	♈	♏	♐	
1	20	17	4	4	8	25	S. 3
6	25	17	4	7	11	♑2	N. 2
11	♑1	18	3	9	15	10	5
16	6	18	3	12	20	18	3
21	11	19	2	15	24	26	S. 3
26	16	19	2	18	29	♒4	5

D.	☽ [illegible]ſe	☽ ſou.	T.
1	2 M 29	8 M. 3	11
2	3 29	8 50	11
3	4 24	9 36	12
4	5 23	10 24	1
5	Moon	11 12	2
6	ſets	12 0	3
7	A.	A. 47	3
8	6 34	1 32	4
9	7 31	2 18	5
10	8 29	3 2	6
11	9 30	3 46	6
12	10 35	4 32	7
13	11 39	5 17	8
14	12 46	6 2	9
15	M. 46	6 48	9
16	1 44	7 44	10
17	2 55	8 40	11
18	4 10	9 41	12
19	5 15	10 43	1
20	Moon	11 45	2
21	riſes	12 47	3
22	A.	M. 47	3
23	7 42	1 45	4
24	8 52	2 39	5
25	10 2	3 28	6
26	11 7	4 12	7
27	12 8	4 56	7
28	M. 8	5 40	8
29	1 0	6 24	9
30	2 0	7 12	10
31	2 55	8 0	11

Five Hundred and Seventy-ſix noble Anceſtors. Carry the Reckoning back 300 Years farther, and the Number amounts to above 500 Millions; which are more than exiſt at any one Time upon upon Earth, and ſhews the Impoſſibility of preſerving Blood free from ſuch Mixtures, and that the Pretenſion of ſuch Purity of Blood in ancient Families is a mere Joke. Hence we ſee how it happens that every Nation has a kind of general Caſt of Feature, by which it may be diſtinguiſhed; continual Intermarriages for a Courſe of Ages rendring all the People related by Blood, and, as it were, of one Family.

On the 6th of this Month, 1711. died in *England*, Mrs. *Jane Sc͏hrimſhaw*, aged 127 Years:--- But *England* boaſts ſome much longer Livers. *James Sands*, of *Horburn*, in the County of *Stafford*, near *Birmingham*, lived 140 Years, and his Wife 120, in a perfect State of Health till the Day of their Deaths. He out-liv'd 5 Leaſes of 21 Years each, all made after his Marriage. *Thomas Parr*, married his firſt Wife at 80 Years of Age, by whom he had two Children; his ſecond Wife after he was 120 Years old, by whom he had one Child, and lived till he was ſomething above 150. *Henry Jenkins*, of the Pariſh of *Balton*, in *Yorkſhire*, died the 8th of this ſame Month, 1670, aged 169 Years. In theſe *American* Parts we have no ſuch very old Men; not that the Climate is unhealthy, but becauſe the preſent Inhabitants *were not born ſoon enough*.

POOR RICHARD'S ALMANACK 1751

Words may show a man's Wit,
but actions his Meaning.

No gains without pains.

It's the easiest thing in the World
for a Man to deceive himself.

Beware of little Expenses,
a small Leak will sink a great Ship.

He who multiplies Riches multiplies Cares.

How many observe Christ's Birthday!
How few, his Precepts!
'Tis easier to keep Holidays than Commandments.

It's common for men to give six pretended reasons instead of one real one.

Dost thou Love life?
Then do not squander Time;
for that's the Stuff Life is made of.

You may talk too much on the best of subjects.

In Rivers and bad Governments,
the lightest Things swim at top.

Good Sense is a Thing all need, few have,
and none think they want.

When the Well's dry,
we know the worth of Water.

Great Good-nature, without Prudence,
is a great Misfortune.

Doing an Injury puts you below your Enemy;
Revenging one makes you but even with him;
Forgiving it sets you above him.

There are lazy Minds as well as lazy Bodies.

If we lose our Money, it gives us some
Concern. If we are cheated or robbed of it,
we are angry: But Money lost may be found;
what we are robbed of may be restored: the
Treasure of Time once lost, can never be
recovered; yet we squander it as though it
were nothing worth, or we had no Use for it.

We may give Advice,
but we cannot give Conduct.

Glass, China, and Reputation, are easily crack'd,
and never well mended.

Hide not your Talents,
they for Use were made.
What's a Sun-Dial in the Shade!

For Age and Want save while you may;
No Morning Sun lasts a whole Day.

Love your Neighbour;
yet don't pull down your Hedge.

Not to oversee Workmen,
is to leave them your purse open.

For want of a Nail the Shoe is lost;
for want of a Shoe, the Horse is lost;
for want of a Horse, the Rider is lost.

Kings have long Arms, but Misfortune longer.
Let none think themselves out of her Reach.

A full Belly makes a dull Brain.

Ambition to be greater and richer, merely
that a Man may have it in his Power to do
more Service to his Friends and the Public,
is of a quiet orderly Kind, pleased if it
succeeds, resigned if it fails. But the
Ambition that has itself only in View, is
restless, turbulent, regardless of public
Peace, or general Interest, and the secret
Maker of most Mischiefs, between Nations,
Parties, Friends and Neighbours.

A long Life may not be good enough,
but a good Life is long enough.

A Change of Fortune hurts a wise Man
no more than a Change of the Moon.

War with your Vices, at Peace with your Neighbours,
and let New Year find you a better Man.

Bad Gains are truly Losses.

What's more valuable than Gold?
Diamonds. Than Diamonds? Virtue.

Neglect mending a small Fault,
and 'twill soon be a great One.

'Tis great Confidence in a Friend
to tell him your Faults,
greater to tell him his.

Diligence overcomes Difficulties,
Sloth makes them.

You may be too cunning for One,
But not for All.

Serving God is Doing Good to Man,
but Praying is thought an easier Service,
and therefore generally chosen.

The first Mistake in public Business,
is the going into it.

Virtue may not always make a Face handsome,
but Vice will certainly make it ugly.

...the Taxes are indeed very heavy, and if
those laid on by the Government were the
only Ones we had to pay, we might more
easily discharge them; but we have many
others, and much more grievous to some of
us. We are taxed twice as much by our
Idleness, three times as much by our Pride,
and four times as much by our Folly, and
from these Taxes the Commissioners cannot
ease or deliver us by allowing an Abatement.

If you would reap Praise you must sow the Seeds,
Gentle Words and useful Deeds.

Learning is a valuable Thing in the Affairs of this Life,
but of infinitely more Importance is Godliness,
as it tends not only to make us happy here but hereafter.

The Honey is sweet;
but the Bee has a Sting.

Speak little, do much.

Some make Conscience of
wearing a Hat in the Church,
who make none of
robbing the Altar.

The learned Fool writes his Nonsense
in better Language than the unlearned;
but still 'tis Nonsense.

'Tis easier to suppress the first Desire
than to satisfy all that follow it.

Nothing brings more pain than too much pleasure;
nothing more bondage than too much liberty.

No longer virtuous no longer free.

Man's tongue is soft, and bone doth lack;
Yet a stroke therewith may break a man's back.

Learning to the Studious;
Riches to the Careful;
Power to the Bold;
Heaven to the Virtuous.

Trouble springs from Idleness;
Toil from Ease.

Want of Care does us more Damage
than Want of Knowledge.

Nothing dries sooner than a Tear.

In studying Law or Physics, or any other
Art or Science, by which you propose to get
your Livelihood, though you find it at first
hard, difficult and unpleasing, use Diligence,
Patience and Perseverance; the Irksomness of
your Task will thus diminish daily, and your
Labour shall finally be crowned with Success.

A brother may not be a friend,
a Friend will always be a Brother.

Many a Man's own Tongue gives
Evidence against his Understanding.

The Brave and the Wise can
both pity and excuse;
when Cowards and fools show no Mercy.

He that carries a small Crime easily,
will carry it on when it comes to be an Ox.

When you're good to others,
you are best to yourself.

When Prosperity was well mounted,
she let go the Bridle,
and soon came tumbling out of the Saddle.

You may delay,
but Time will not.

'Tis easier to build two Chimneys,
than maintain one in Fuel.

He that would rise at Court,
must begin by Creeping.

Many a Man would have been worse,
if his Estate had been better.

Robbers must exalted be,
Small ones on the Gallow-Tree,
While greater ones descend to Thrones.

Great modesty often hides great Merit.

So what signifies wishing and
hoping for better Times.
We may make these Times
better if we better ourselves.

The royal Crown cures not the Head-ach.

HOW TO MAKE A STRIKING SUNDIAL

How to make a Striking Sundial, by which not only a Man's own Family, but all his Neighbours for ten Miles round, may know what a Clock it is, when the Sun shines, without seeing the Dial.

Choose an open Place in your Yard or Garden, on which the Sun may shine all Day without any Impediment from Trees or Buildings. On the Ground mark out your Hour Liner, as for a horizontal Dial, according to Art, taking Room enough for the Guns On the Line for One o'Clock, place one Gun; on the Two o'Clock line two Guns, and so of the rest. The Guns must all be charged with Powder, but Ball is unnecessary. Your Gunman or Staff must have twelve burning Glasses annex'd to it, and be so placed as that the Sun shining through the Glasses, one after the other, shall cause the Focus or burning Spot to fall on the Hour Line of One, for Example, at one o'Clock, and there kindle a Train that shall discharge two Guns successively; and so of the rest.

Note, There must be 78 Guns in all. Thirty-two Pounders will be best for this Use; but 18 Pounders may do, and will cost less, as well as use less Powder, for nine Pounds of Powder will do for one Charge of each eighteen Pounder, whereas the Thirty-two Pounders would require for each Gun 16 Pounds.

Note also, That the chief Expence will be the Powder, for the Cannon once bought, will, with Care, last 100 Years.

Note moreover, That there will be a great Saving of Powder in cloudy Days.

Kind Reader, Methinks I hear thee say, That it is indeed a good Thing to know how the Time passes, but this Kind of Dial, notwithstanding the mentioned Savings, would be very expensive; and the Cost greater than the Advantage. Thou art wise, my Friend, to be so considerate beforehand; some Fools would not have found out so much, till they had made the Dial and try'd it.---Let all such learn that many a private and many a publick Project, are like this Striking Dial, great Cost for little Profit.

Little Strokes, Fell great Oaks.

Genius without Education
is like Silver in the Mine.

Though I Beauty admire,
'tis VIRTUE I prize,
Which fades not in seventy Years.

Industry pays debts, Despair increases them.

Scarlet, Silk, and Velvet, have put
out the Kitchen Fire.

He that lives well, is learned enough.

The poor have little, beggars none,
the rich too much, enough not one.

The excellency of hogs is fatness, of men virtue.

He that would catch Fish,
must venture his Bait.

Clean your Finger,
before you point at my Spots.

A good Example is the best sermon.

There are three Things extreamly hard,
Steel, a Diamond, and to know one's self.

Content makes poor men rich;
Discontent makes rich Men poor.

Some antient Philosophers have said, that
Happiness depends more on the inward
Disposition of Mind than on outward
Circumstances; and that he who cannot be
happy in any State, can be so in no State. To
be happy, they tell us we must be content.
Right. But they do not teach how we may
become content. Poor Richard shall give
you a short good Rule for that. To be
content, look backward on those who
possess less than yourself, not forward on
those who possess more. If this does not
make you content, you don't deserve to be
happy.

Other books by

Blue Mountain Arts inc.

Come Into the Mountains, Dear Friend
by Susan Polis Schutz
I Want to Laugh, I Want to Cry
by Susan Polis Schutz
Peace Flows from the Sky
by Susan Polis Schutz
Someone Else to Love
by Susan Polis Schutz

The Best Is Yet to Be
The International Grandmothers' Cookbook
Step to the Music You Hear, Vol. I
Step to the Music You Hear, Vol. II
The Desiderata of Happiness
The Language of Friendship
The Language of Love
Whatever Is, Is Best
I Care About Your Happiness
My Life and Love Are One